Do You Know Your Wine?

The Ultimate European Wine Quiz

Author Val Policella

ISBN: 1976052580
ISBN-13: 978-1976052583

Do You Know Your Wine?

CONTENTS

Introduction

This book is a collection of wine quizzes for amateur wine enthusiasts designed to test your knowledge of wines and wine related trivia by country of origin.

I have had several great evenings with family and friends over the years whilst sharing a fabulous bottle of wine or two!

Why not open a bottle or two with friends and family or host your own wine evening, pick up this book, put your quizmaster's hat on and away you go.

Included within this book is a section for recording your own personal wine tasting notes and recording your personal favourite wines.

I hope you enjoy these quizzes as much as I have.

Do You Know Your Wine?

FRANCE

1. How many wine regions are there in
    France?
    A. 13
    B. 17
    C. 19

2. Which dinner course would a Sauternes
    wine typically be served with?

3. Which wine growing region is the City
    of Reims situated in?

4. Which grape is Beaujolais usually made
    from?

5. Which French wine region is an island
    in the Mediterranean?

6. When is Beaujolais Nouveau released
    for general sale?

7. Which grape is the most widely planted
    white grape variety in France?

8. Where does this white grape variety (answer number 7) originate from?

9. Which is the largest wine producing region in France?

10. What type of wine is primarily produced in the Alsace region?

VAL POLICELLA

GERMANY

1. What is the name given to the wine produced from grapes that have been frozen on the vine?

2. What is the German name for the wine translated as "Beloved lady's milk"?

3. What does the word "Trocken" mean on a wine label?

4. White wine accounts for how much of the total wine production in Germany?

   A. 3/4

   B. 1/2

   C. 2/3

5. What is the German name for Pinot Noir?

6. What is German sparkling wine better

known as?

7. Which grape of German origin is the most planted variety of grape in Germany?

8. Is the Dornfelder grape used for making red or white wine?

9. Along which river is the main wine growing area in Germany?

10. Which direction do the vineyards face?

A. North

B. East

C. South

D. West

Do You Know Your Wine?

SPAIN

1. Which grape variety is most commonly used for making Rioja?

   A. Zinfandel

   B. Pinot Grigio

   C. Tempranillo

2. How many categories are there for Rioja red wines?

   A. 3

   B. 4

   C. 5

3. What is the name given to Spanish sparkling wine?

4. Which type of Spanish wine is classed as "Fino"?

5. What is the minimum length of time

that a Rioja Reserva red wine must be aged?

6. What is the Spanish word for winery?

7. The majority of Spanish Cava is produced in which area of Catalonia?

8. What does "vino tinto de mesa" translate as?

9. Old Sherry casks are sold to be used for ageing which spirit?

10. How many varieties of grape are grown in Spain for Sherry production?

   A. 3

   B. 12

   C. 74

VAL POLICELLA

ITALY

1. Which Italian white grape is also the name for an Italian hard cheese?

    A. Fiano

    B. Pecorino

    C. Pigato

2. Which type of wine is Asti Spumante?

    A. White

    B. Red

    C. Sparkling

3. How many wine growing regions does Italy have?

    A. 16

    B. 20

    C. 21

4. Which of the Italian wine growing

regions is the most southerly?

5. Which Italian wine is associated with Hannibal Lecter?

6. What are the two best known wines from the Piedmont region?

7. Which is the most widely planted red grape in Italy?

8. What is the name of an Italian red wine grape and a wine made primarily from this grape?

9. Which region is Soave from?

10. What is the name of an Italian wine linked with this quiz book?

Do You Know Your Wine?

PORTUGAL

1. Which city does Port get its name from?

2. Which fortified wine is made on the islands of the same name?

3. On a bottle of Portuguese wine, what does the word "Doce" mean?

4. Colares wine is made from vines grown in which type of soil?

   A. Clay based soil

   B. Silt soil

   C. Sandy soil

5. What is the minimum length of time a Madeira wine must be aged before it can be classed as Vintage?

   A. 15 years

   B. 20 years

C. 25 years

6. How many sub regions are there within the Vinho Verde region?

7. What is the Portuguese word for vineyard?

8. For what reason is the word vintage not allowed to appear on bottles of vintage Madeira?

9. Traditionally in the United Kingdom at a formal dinner, which way round the table should the Port be passed?

10. Which is the most westerly Portuguese wine region?

VAL POLICELLA

UNITED KINGDOM

1. In the United Kingdom, which grape is also known as Wrotham Pinot?

2. Which grape variety is most widely planted in the United Kingdom?

3. Who introduced wine in to England?

4. What percentage of wine production in the United Kingdom is sparkling wine?

    A. 15%

    B. 38%

    C. 66%

5. Chardonnay, Pinot Meunier and which other grape variety account for over fifty percent of plantings for the production of sparkling wine?

6. Which year was the first commercial vineyard planted in Wales?

7. Which type of wine is primarily
    produced in Wales?

    A. Red

    B. White

    C. Sparkling

8. In which county is the largest vineyard
    in the United Kingdom situated?

9. In which year was England's oldest
    commercial vineyard established?

10. British wine accounts for how much of
    domestic wine sales in the United
    Kingdom?

    A. 1%

    B. 7%

    C. 13%

Do You Know Your Wine?

BULGARIA

1. How many wine regions are there in Bulgaria?

2. Red wine grape varieties account for how much of the vines grown in Bulgaria?

   A. 31%

   B. 47%

   C. 63%

3. The Dimyat grape produces which type of wine?

   A. Sparkling

   B. White

   C. Red

4. 30% of the vines growing in Bulgaria are located in which region?

5. True or false? Bulgaria is the 2nd largest

bottled wine exporter in the world.

6. Which wine region is the Mavrud grape from?

7. Which former Prime Minister of the United Kingdom was known to have an annual order of 500 litres of Bulgarian Melnik wine?

8. How many wineries are in the Thracian Valley?

9. True or false? In the 1980s Bulgaria was the 2nd largest wine producer in the world.

10. The Sungurlare Valley is famous for its wine made from which grape variety?

VAL POLICELLA

GREECE

1. Which Greek wine is the national drink of Greece?

2. In which year was Greece's 1st Cabernet Sauvignon vineyard planted?

   A. 1958

   B. 1961

   C. 1963

3. How many wine regions are there in Greece?

4. Which white wine grape is primarily grown in the Epirus region?

5. What is Retsina flavoured with?

6. Which type of wine is produced from the Kotsifali grape?

   A. Red

   B. White

   C. Sparkling

7. Which wine from Santorini shares its name with a sweet Italian Tuscan wine?

8. In which year was The Wine Institute founded by the Greek Ministry of Agriculture?

9. Which white wine grape variety is mostly grown in the mountain vineyards of Kefalonia?

10. The Savatiano grape is primarily used to produce which wine?

Do You Know Your Wine?

AUSTRIA

1. Which white wine grape variety is most widely used in Austria?

2. The Muscat Ottonel grape is used to produce which type of wine?

    A. Red

    B. Sparkling

    C. Dessert

3. In which year did the Austrian wineries suffer from the "antifreeze scandal"?

4. Which is the largest wine growing area in Austria?

5. In which region is this area (answer number 4) located?

6. Which region produces most of the red wine from Austria?

7. How much of the wine produced in Austria is consumed domestically?

8. How many wine producers are there in the Vienna wine region?

   A. 47

   B. 239

   C. 630

9. Which is the most widely grown red grape variety in Austria?

10. How many white wine grape varieties are classified for the production of wine in Austria?

VAL POLICELLA

ROMANIA

1. Romania is one of the largest wine producers in the world. How do they rank amongst European wine producers?

   A. 3rd

   B. 6th

   C. 8th

2. How do they rank amongst the World wine producers?

   A. 8th

   B. 11th

   C. 13th

3. The Fetească Alba grape produces which type of wine?

   A. Sparkling

   B. Red

C. White

4. How much alcohol content would you expect a Fetească Neagră grape wine to be?

A. 7-11%

B. 12-14%

C. 13-15%

5. True or false? The county of Vrancea is the largest wine producer in Romania.

6. How much area of Vrancea County is covered with vines?

A. 11%

B. 16%

C. 23%

7. Which type of wines is the Panciu region famous for?

8. What does "Vin de Masa" translate as?

9. The Murfatlar region produces several types of wine, but which type of wine is

it most famous for?

A. Dry

B. Medium

C. Sweet

10. Which is the smallest wine growing region in Romania?

36

PERSONAL WINE TASTING NOTES

VAL POLICELLA

Do You Know Your Wine?

VAL POLICELLA

Do You Know Your Wine?

PERSONAL FAVOURITE WINES

VAL POLICELLA

Do You Know Your Wine?

VAL POLICELLA

VAL POLICELLA

QUIZ ANSWERS

FRANCE

1. 13

2. Dessert

3. Champagne

4. Gamay grape

5. Corsica

6. The third Thursday of November

7. Ugni Blanc

8. Italy

9. Languedoc-Roussillon

10. White wine

GERMANY

1. Eiswein

2. Liebfraumilch

3. Dry

4. 2/3

5. Spätburgunder

6. Sekt

7. Riesling

8. Red

9. Rhine

10. South

SPAIN

1. Tempranillo

2. 4

3. Cava

4. Sherry

5. 3 years including a minimum 1 year in oak barrels

6. Winery

7. Penedès

8. Red table wine

9. Whisky

10. 3

ITALY

1. Pecorino

2. Sparkling

3. 20

4. Sicily

5. Chianti

6. Barolo and Barbaresco

7. Sangiovese

8. Lambrusco

9. Veneto

10. Valpolicella

PORTUGAL

1. Porto

2. Madeira

3. Sweet

4. Sandy soil

5. 20

6. 9

7. Quinta

8. It's a trademark belonging to Port producers

9. To the left

10. Azores

UNITED KINGDOM

1. Pinot Meunier

2. Chardonnay

3. The Romans

4. 66%

5. Pinot Noir

6. 1875

7. White

8. Surrey

9. 1952

10. 1%

BULGARIA

1. 5

2. 63%

3. White

4. Black sea region (East Bulgarian)

5. True

6. Thracian Lowland

7. Winston Churchill

8. 12

9. True

10. Red Misket

GREECE

1. Retsina

2. 1963

3. 7

4. Debina

5. Pine resin

6. Red

7. Vin Santo

8. 1937

9. Robola

10. Retsina

AUSTRIA

1. Grüner Veltliner

2. Dessert

3. 1985

4. Weinviertel

5. Lower Austria

6. Burgenland

7. 75%

8. 630

9. Zweigelt

10. 22

ROMANIA

1. 6th

2. 13th

3. White

4. 12-14%

5. True

6. 11%

7. White wines and sparkling wines

8. Table wine

9. Sweet

10. Banat

Do You Know Your Wine?